Francis Frith's
SEVENOAKS & TONBRIDGE

PHOTOGRAPHIC MEMORIES

Francis Frith's
SEVENOAKS & TONBRIDGE

◆

Helen Livingston

FRITH
BOOK Co

First published in the United Kingdom in 1999 by
Frith Book Company Ltd

Hardback Edition 1999
ISBN 1-85937-057-8

Paperback Edition 2001
ISBN 1-85937-392-5

British Library Cataloguing in Publication Data

Francis Frith's Sevenoaks and Tonbridge
Helen Livingston

Frith Book Company Ltd
Frith's Barn, Teffont,
Salisbury, Wiltshire SP3 5QP
Tel: +44 (0) 1722 716 376
Email: info@francisfrith.co.uk
www.francisfrith.co.uk

Printed and bound in Great Britain

AS WITH ANY HISTORICAL DATABASE THE FRITH ARCHIVE IS CONSTANTLY BEING CORRECTED AND IMPROVED
AND THE PUBLISHERS WOULD WELCOME INFORMATION ON OMISSIONS OR INACCURACIES

CONTENTS

FRANCIS FRITH: *Victorian Pioneer*

FRANCIS FRITH, Victorian founder of the world-famous photographic archive, was a complex and multitudinous man. A devout Quaker and a highly successful Victorian businessman, he was both philosophic by nature and pioneering in outlook.

By 1855 Francis Frith had already established a wholesale grocery business in Liverpool, and sold it for the astonishing sum of £200,000, which is the equivalent today of over £15,000,000. Now a multi-millionaire, he was able to indulge his passion for travel. As a child he had pored over travel books written by early explorers, and his fancy and imagination had been stirred by family holidays to the sublime mountain regions of Wales and Scotland. 'What a land of spirit-stirring and enriching scenes and places!' he had written. He was to return to these scenes of grandeur in later years to 'recapture the thousands of vivid and tender memories', but with a different purpose. Now in his thirties, and captivated by the new science of photography, Frith set out on a series of pioneering journeys to the Nile regions that occupied him from 1856 until 1860.

INTRIGUE AND ADVENTURE

He took with him on his travels a specially-designed wicker carriage that acted as both dark-room and sleeping chamber. These far-flung journeys were packed with intrigue and adventure. In his life story, written when he was sixty-three, Frith tells of being held captive by bandits, and of fighting 'an awful midnight battle to the very point of surrender with a deadly pack of hungry, wild dogs'. Sporting flowing Arab costume, Frith arrived at Akaba by camel seventy years before Lawrence, where he encountered 'desert princes and rival sheikhs, blazing with jewel-hilted swords'.

During these extraordinary adventures he was assiduously exploring the desert regions bordering the Nile and patiently recording the antiquities and peoples with his camera. He was the first photographer to venture beyond the sixth cataract. Africa was still the mysterious 'Dark Continent', and Stanley and Livingstone's historic meeting was a decade into the future. The conditions for picture taking confound belief. He laboured for hours in his wicker dark-room in the sweltering heat of the desert, while the volatile chemicals fizzed dangerously in their trays. Often he was forced to work in remote tombs and caves where conditions were cooler. Back in London he exhibited his photographs and was 'rapturously cheered' by members of the Royal Society. His reputation as a photographer was made overnight. An eminent modern historian has likened their impact on the population of the time to that on our own generation of the first photographs taken on the surface of the moon.

VENTURE OF A LIFE-TIME

Characteristically, Frith quickly spotted the opportunity to create a new business as a specialist publisher of photographs. He lived in an era of immense and sometimes violent change. For the poor in the early part of Victoria's reign work was a drudge and the hours long, and people had precious little free time to enjoy themselves.

Most had no transport other than a cart or gig at their disposal, and had not travelled far beyond the boundaries of their own town or village. However, by the 1870s, the railways had threaded their way across the country, and Bank Holidays and half-day Saturdays had been made obligatory by Act of Parliament. All of a sudden the ordinary working man and his family were able to enjoy days out and see a little more of the world.

With characteristic business acumen, Francis Frith foresaw that these new tourists would enjoy having souvenirs to commemorate their days out. In 1860 he married Mary Ann Rosling and set out with the intention of photographing every city, town and village in Britain. For the next thirty years he travelled the country by train and by pony and trap, producing fine photographs of seaside resorts and beauty spots that were keenly bought by millions of Victorians. These prints were painstakingly pasted into family albums and pored over during the dark nights of winter, rekindling precious memories of summer excursions.

THE RISE OF FRITH & CO

Frith's studio was soon supplying retail shops all over the country. To meet the demand he gathered about him a small team of photographers, and published the work of independent artist-photographers of the calibre of Roger Fenton and Francis Bedford. In order to gain some understanding of the scale of Frith's business one only has to look at the catalogue issued by Frith & Co in 1886: it runs to some 670

pages, listing not only many thousands of views of the British Isles but also many photographs of most European countries, and China, Japan, the USA and Canada – note the sample page shown above from the hand-written *Frith & Co* ledgers detailing pictures taken. By 1890 Frith had created the greatest specialist photographic publishing company in the world, with over 2,000 outlets – more than the combined number that Boots and WH Smith have today! The picture on the right shows the *Frith & Co* display board at Ingleton in the Yorkshire Dales. Beautifully constructed with mahogany frame and gilt inserts, it could display up to a dozen local scenes.

POSTCARD BONANZA

◆◆

The ever-popular holiday postcard we know today took many years to develop. In 1870 the Post Office issued the first plain cards, with a pre-printed stamp on one face. In 1894 they allowed other publishers' cards to be sent through the mail with an attached adhesive halfpenny stamp. Demand grew rapidly, and in 1895 a new size of postcard was permitted called the

court card, but there was little room for illustration. In 1899, a year after Frith's death, a new card measuring 5.5 x 3.5 inches became the standard format, but it was not until 1902 that the divided back came into being, with address and message on one face and a full-size illustration on the other. *Frith & Co* were in the vanguard of postcard development, and Frith's sons Eustace and Cyril continued their father's monumental task, expanding the number of views offered to the public and recording more and more places in Britain, as the coasts and countryside were opened up to mass travel.

Francis Frith died in 1898 at his villa in Cannes, his great project still growing. The archive he created continued in business for another seventy years. By 1970 it contained over a third of a million pictures of 7,000 cities, towns and villages. The massive photographic record Frith has left to us stands as a living monument to a special and very remarkable man.

Frith's Archive: *A Unique Legacy*

FRANCIS FRITH'S legacy to us today is of immense significance and value, for the magnificent archive of evocative photographs he created provides a unique record of change in 7,000 cities, towns and villages throughout Britain over a century and more. Frith and his fellow studio photographers revisited locations many times down the years to update their views, compiling for us an enthralling and colourful pageant of British life and character.

We tend to think of Frith's sepia views of Britain as nostalgic, for most of us use them to conjure up memories of places in our own lives with which we have family associations. It often makes us forget that to Francis Frith they were records of daily life as it was actually being lived in the cities, towns and villages of his day. The Victorian age was one of great and often bewildering change for ordinary people, and though the pictures evoke an impression of slower times, life was as busy and hectic as it is today.

We are fortunate that Frith was a photographer of the people, dedicated to recording the minutiae of everyday life. For it is this sheer wealth of visual data, the painstaking chronicle of changes in dress, transport, street layouts, buildings, housing, engineering and landscape that captivates us so much today. His remarkable images offer us a powerful link with the past and with the lives of our ancestors.

TODAY'S TECHNOLOGY

Computers have now made it possible for Frith's many thousands of images to be accessed almost instantly. In the Frith archive today, each photograph is carefully 'digitised' then stored on a CD Rom. Frith archivists can locate a single photograph amongst thousands within seconds. Views can be catalogued and sorted under a variety of categories of place and content to the immediate benefit of researchers. Inexpensive reference prints can be created for them at the touch of a mouse button, and a wide range of books and other printed materials assembled and published for a wider, more general readership - in the next twelve months over a hundred Frith local history titles will be published! The

See Frith at www.francisfrith.co.uk

day-to-day workings of the archive are very different from how they were in Francis Frith's time: imagine the herculean task of sorting through eleven tons of glass negatives as Frith had to do to locate a particular sequence of pictures! Yet the archive still prides itself on maintaining the same high standards of excellence laid down by Francis Frith, including the painstaking cataloguing and indexing of every view.

It is curious to reflect on how the internet now allows researchers in America and elsewhere greater instant access to the archive than Frith himself ever enjoyed. Many thousands of individual views can be called up on screen within seconds on one of the Frith internet sites, enabling people living continents away to revisit the streets of their ancestral home town, or view places in Britain where they have enjoyed holidays. Many overseas researchers welcome the chance to view special theme selections, such as transport, sports, costume and ancient monuments.

We are certain that Francis Frith would have heartily approved of these modern developments, for he himself was always working at the very limits of Victorian photographic technology.

THE VALUE OF THE ARCHIVE TODAY

Because of the benefits brought by the computer, Frith's images are increasingly studied by social historians, by researchers into genealogy and ancestory, by architects, town planners, and by teachers and schoolchildren involved in local history projects. In addition, the archive offers every one of us a unique opportunity to examine the places where we and our families have lived and worked down the years. Immensely successful in Frith's own era, the archive is now, a century and more on, entering a new phase of popularity.

THE PAST IN TUNE WITH THE FUTURE

Historians consider the Francis Frith Collection to be of prime national importance. It is the only archive of its kind remaining in private ownership and has been valued at a million pounds. However, this figure is now rapidly increasing as digital technology enables more and more people around the world to enjoy its benefits.

Francis Frith's archive is now housed in an historic timber barn in the beautiful village of Teffont in Wiltshire. Its founder would not recognize the archive office as it is today. In place of the many thousands of dusty boxes containing glass plate negatives and an all-pervading odour of photographic chemicals, there are now ranks of computer screens. He would be amazed to watch his images travelling round the world at unimaginable speeds through network and internet lines.

The archive's future is both bright and exciting. Francis Frith, with his unshakeable belief in making photographs available to the greatest number of people, would undoubtedly approve of what is being done today with his lifetime's work. His photographs, depicting our shared past, are now bringing pleasure and enlightenment to millions around the world a century and more after his death.

Sevenoaks & Tonbridge
– An Introduction

SEVENOAKS AND TONBRIDGE are both main-street towns separated by some six miles of Kent countryside. The road which links them is of no great antiquity and probably dates only from Saxon times. It was part of the Norman and Medieval route from London to the Channel ports of Hastings, Rye and Winchelsea, and once proudly bore the names of the Hastings Road and in Tudor times, the Rye Road. Later, in pre-by-pass days, it was the A21. Tradition claims it as the road along which Harold marched to meet William of Normandy at the Battle of Hastings. It was the first road in Kent to be turnpiked, an event which took place in 1710. This turnpike road ran from Sevenoaks through Tonbridge to Pembury, carrying fashionable visitors to the spa town of Tunbridge Wells. Though originally founded for different reasons, Sevenoaks as a market and Tonbridge as a defensive crossing point with a mighty castle on the River Medway, these towns both grew along their respective main streets, and even today that pattern is noticeable. In the 18th and 19th centuries both were post towns on the road and it was the road taken by the fish catch from Rye - from 1761 the Rye fish carriers paid reduced turnpike tolls. Today both towns are busy commercial centres known for their schools.

SEVENOAKS

Sevenoaks stands some 500-600 feet above sea level on the sandstone hills south of the Vale of Holmesdale, looking northwards over the vale to the chalky North Downs, and southwards to the heathy heights of the High Weald and Ashdown Forest. It is not known exactly when the first houses were built at Sevenoaks, but it was almost certainly during Saxon times, when they would have sprung up as a small roadside settlement, serving the needs of travellers. We know that a church existed at Sevenoaks in 1122, and it seems reasonable to assume that the first settlement was built here during the preceding centuries, perhaps during the time of Alfred the Great. Historically, nearby Otford was of far greater importance, and in AD 791 Offa granted the manor of Otford to the Archbishop of Canterbury. The extensive lands of Otford manor stretched from the North Downs near Shoreham southwards to Tonbridge and included the future site of Sevenoaks.

The town's name really does seem to mean seven oak trees, which is a very unusual type of place name for a settlement of Saxon origin. These trees probably grew near the present site of the church - the most likely spot for the first tiny settlement here, a mere halting place for travellers - and they probably grew in a clump, not in a straight line. The clump of trees marking the wayside houses is likely to have been visible for some distance and thus

tion of the original oaks. The tradition of seven oak trees planted in a straight line along the main road to the south of the town dates only from the 18th century. The tradition of seven oak tees on the northern perimeter of the Vine is even younger. The original oaks on the Vine were planted to celebrate the accession of Edward VII. Sadly six of them were felled by the 1987 hurricane, but they have been replanted.

Sevenoaks began to grow noticeably during the 13th century when the market was founded. It seems that the original market place was on Upper High Street outside the present Chequers Inn. Later it was moved to

christened the settlement. They had vanished by medieval times, fallen or felled, consumed as building timber or as firewood, but leaving their shadowy presence in the name they bequeathed to the little town. Nowhere in all the documentation of Sevenoaks in the Middle Ages do oak trees get a mention. The Elizabethan William Lambarde suggests the derivation of the name as 'of a number of trees as they conjecture', showing that in 1570 there was no tradition to point out the loca-

the Y-shaped road junction where the fountain now stands. Here the easterly branch of the Y heads off for Dartford along the High Street, and the London road continues along the western branch. Markets were held on Saturdays, fairs on St Nicholas' Day (6th December) and St Peter's Day (29th June). Sevenoaks' market was originally for cattle driven to town on the hoof from the surrounding farms. The Shambles was a jumble of buildings that grew up between the arms of the Y-junction. It was originally an area that served the market, full of slaughter houses and butchers' shops. There was once a market cross, but this has disappeared from the face of the earth. It probably stood on the site of the Market Hall.

Until the coming of the railways in 1862 and 1868 Sevenoaks drew much of its life from the road. It was an important, self contained town on the highway, with coaches running hither and thither to destinations such as London and the coast from its old coaching inns, notably the Chequers and the Royal Oak (formerly the Black Bull). When the railway arrived Sevenoaks came within the pull of London, and changed from being 'a very genteel little town' (as the 1839 Guide described it) to being a high-class London dormitory. Large Victorian villas went up, as did smaller houses and terraces, and the atmosphere of the town was never the same again. The town has spread and grown ever since, with continued building right up to the present, and the population is now about 18,500 souls.

An important side effect of the coming of the railway was the provision of the town with a proper water supply. Until then water was available at specific points of the town, but problems with flooding on the railway prompted a use to be found for the water. One of the original town pumps can still be seen at the foot of Six Bells Lane.

Sevenoaks' one great historical event was the Battle of Sole Fields in 1450, when the rebel Jack Cade and his band of followers defeated a contingent of the king's army under Sir Humphrey Stafford. The battlefield lay between the town and Sevenoaks Weald, the little village to the south, and is now built over. Nearly five hundred years later, during the First and Second World Wars, Sevenoaks saw thousands of troops stationed in the town on their way to the battlefields of Europe, while wounded soldiers brought back from the front were nursed in the town's hospitals.

The parish church of St Nicholas dates mainly from the 15th century but probably stands on the site of an earlier church of Norman, possibly Saxon, age. It has been heavily restored and in 1947 its roof was burned out.

Sevenoaks School was founded under the will of William Sevenoak (or Sennoke) who died in 1432. This remarkable man was, according to tradition, a foundling of the town. Rescued from destitution, he rose to be a wealthy grocer and Mayor of London in 1418-19. He was friend and contemporary of the great Sir Richard Whittington. It is even said that he accompanied Henry V to France, fought at Agincourt and vanquished the Dauphin in single combat. Under his will he endowed some almshouses and 'a Grammar School' for poor boys, stipulating, most unusually for those days, that the master should not be a priest.

The Vine, the triangular-shaped open space on the north of the town, is one of the oldest of all cricket grounds. It was given to the town by the 3rd Duke of Dorset in 1773 'to be a cricket ground for ever'.

Knole is the greatest of the great houses of Sevenoaks, though it remains remarkably distinct from the town, set in its magnificent 1,000 acre deer park. This means that to the east the distinction between town and country is far more abrupt than is usual today. Knole is named from the knoll on which it stands, a huge Tudor and Jacobean mansion which replaced the original medieval manor house. Elizabeth I gave it to Thomas Sackville who was created Earl of Dorset under James I. It is still the home of the Sackvilles, though it is now owned by the National Trust.

The most famous family associated with Sevenoaks is undoubtedly the Sackvilles of Knole, later the Dukes of Dorset. Victoria (Vita) Sackville-West was born and grew up at Knole. None the less, other famous people are connected with the town. William Sevenoke, founder of Sevenoaks School and onetime Mayor of London, has already been mentioned, as has William Lambarde. He was author of the 'Perambulation of Kent', the

Sevenoaks. She stayed with her great uncle at his home, the Red House, in Upper High Street.

These photographs charmingly represent a small Kentish market town from before the era of the motor car up to the prosperous 1970s.

TONBRIDGE

Tonbridge - pronounced and in earlier days spelled 'Tun-bridge' - occupies the flat meadowlands of the Medway valley. The town grew beside the moated Norman castle originally built in William the Conqueror's time by

first county topography ever to be written. This was published in 1570. Lambarde is buried at Sevenoaks and came from a Sevenoaks family, although he was born in London and died at Greenwich. The poet John Donne was rector of St Nicholas' church from 1616 till his death in 1631. As was usual in those days, he did not officiate here himself, but appointed a vicar to do his pastoral duties. There is a tablet to him in the chancel. Jane Austen was a frequent visitor to

one of his barons to guard the ford over the Medway on the London to south coast road. The castle builder was Richard de Bienfait, also known as Richard de Tonbridge, whose family later changed their name to de Clare (after their great estate in Suffolk) and who became very considerable landowners. They were also indefatigable castle builders and in the 13th century rebuilt the earlier wooden castle in stone.

The castle had an active life, as its owners

were frequently at odds with the crown. It was besieged by William II in 1088 and captured after only two days. Again, in 1264, it fell to Royal forces after the de Clares had joined Simon de Montfort's faction. Nothing of the great keep which saw this action remains, save the huge earthen motte on which it stood. The keep was used by the Parliamentarians

market lasted until the early years of the 20th century, but the tradition continues today in the colourful Saturday markets.

The original settlement along the High Street to the north of the river is still the most rewarding part of the town. The buildings along this part of High Street are mostly 18th and 19th century, with the occasional 20th

during the great Civil War, and it was dismantled soon afterwards, the stone carted away for reuse elsewhere. The massive 13th century gatehouse still stands, with its round towers and hall on the second floor, as does part of the curtain wall. Alongside the gatehouse is a house of 1793, which is now used as municipal offices, but was built as his home by Mr Hooker, who planted the area within the castle moat with vines. The area is now the pleasant landscaped Castle Gardens.

The town of Tonbridge owes its existence to the former ford and later the bridge which carries the old post road over the river Medway. The town developed northwards along the Sevenoaks road from the castle and river crossing, with a market place at the southern end close to the castle. This cattle

century piece dropped in. The basic layout of the town is fairly simple. High Street runs approximately north - south. Bordyke, the 'borough ditch' or border, enclosed the town to the north, while the River Medway enclosed it to the south.

The River Medway has been of great importance to Tonbridge. A highway from earliest times, its navigation was improved from the 17th century by the addition of locks, though their small size always hampered the use of the river by commercial traffic. The navigation reached Tonbridge in 1741 and, in 1828, it was proposed to extend the navigation upstream to Penshurst. James Christie was engaged as engineer. Anxious to control water rights, he bought the Town Mills at Tonbridge and proceeded to drain the Town Pen, thereby stranding all the barges at the wharves. He was bankrupted by the ensuing court cases.

Tonbridge's location on to the river Medway allowed heavy industries to flourish, including powder mills, corn mills and breweries, with hops and timber passing downstream. It must be remembered that Tonbridge lay within the iron producing region of the Weald and, apart from producing iron goods herself, was responsible for the shipment downstream of many a Sussex cannon and shot destined for the navy. The local gasworks were set up in the 1830s and the town's streets were lit by gas from 12 November 1836. From Victorian times onwards the river has been used for leisure, with boats for hire close to the Big Bridge.

If the Medway helped bring prosperity to Tonbridge, it also brought frequent and occasionally disastrous flooding, as the soils of the clay vale through which it flows are quickly saturated. The most recent bad floods were in 1968. It is now most unlikely that such flooding will ever occur again, for the largest on-river flood storage area in Britain has now been created near Haysden, just upstream of the town. Here flood water can be held back in a temporary lake.

The growth of the town accelerated greatly from 1842 when the railway arrived. Tonbridge became a London dormitory town for well-off businessmen. Industry flourished, with continued emphasis on the heavy industry along the Medway. The 20th century has seen the development of chemical works on the site of the former powder mills and many light industries, including the making of cricket balls. The town now sprawls northwards as well as to the south, with residential as well as industrial estates. Some 34,500 people now live in Tonbridge.

Some medieval buildings survive, notably the Port Reeve's House in East Street and in the High Street, the Chequers Inn and the house next to it, for long a shop. Sadly the adjacent old town hall was demolished as long ago as 1901. This allowed the road to be

widened and the National Westminster Bank was built on part of the site. The Rose and Crown, with its chequered brick facade, is in fact a 16th century timber framed structure. There are several attractive Georgian houses in the town, two of which, Judd House and Ferox Hall, have been taken over by Tonbridge School. The Ivy House Inn on the corner of High Street and Bordyke is one of the oldest hostelries in Tonbridge. It was formerly known as the Elephant.

The church, dedicated to St Peter and St Paul, is a large building with a 13th century nave, and a Norman chancel which was the original church. The north aisle dates from the 14th century and the south aisle from the 19th. The tower was built in the 13th century. The whole fabric was heavily restored in 1879. Nothing remains of the former Priory of St Mary Magdalene, founded south of the river in the 12th century. It was suppressed by Wolsey in 1524 to help fund his planned Cardinal College at Oxford and its site is now occupied by the railway.

Tonbridge is famous for its school, founded 1533 under a bequest of Sir Andrew Judd, a member of the Skinners Company. The oldest extant school buildings, the entrance quadrangle, date from 1760 and were enlarged in 1826. The main block is Victorian gothic dating from 1863 and 1894. The chapel of 1902 was burned down in 1989 but has been lovingly restored. Famous former pupils include Sir Sidney Smith (1764-1840), the novelist E M Forster and the cricketer Colin Cowdrey.

Famous Tonbridge people include the poetess and best selling cookery writer, Eliza Acton (1799-1859). It is said that she tested every recipe she published in her own kitchen. She lived at the Priory in Bordyke. Here at Tonbridge we meet with Jane Austen's family again, for her father, the Reverend George, was for a while a master at Tonbridge School.

These photographs record with loving detail the Tonbridge of yesterday, spanning the years from the late 19th century to the 1960s.

Sevenoaks Town

THE HIGH STREET and other parts of the town of Sevenoaks were pictured by Frith's photographers at the end of the 19th century and again in the middle years of the 20th century. Interestingly, although there are obvious changes wrought by time, the scenes are immediately recognisable. Upper High Street is architecturally the finest part of the town and pictures included here show the early 18th century buildings of Sevenoaks School, set back a little from the road, the tile hung Old Post Office, dating from the 16th century, and the Chantry, an imposing house of about 1700. Here also are pictures of the house at Rayley's Corner, at the junction of Upper High Street and Six Bells Lane. The 'corner' was named after the baker's shop, a timber framed house of 16th century date which itself was originally the Six Bells alehouse. The six bells in question were the original peal of six bells at St Nicholas' parish church.

Views of the Upper High Street include those taken at the Victorian fountain, where London Road and the High Street (the Dartford Road) diverge, in the days both before and after the present Midland Bank was built at the junction. Until the 1920s the building at the junction was the Sevenoaks Coffee Tavern, later the West End Dairy, but was replaced in 1922-23 by the present Midland Bank. On the western side of the fountain stands the half timbered and tile hung former Archbishop's Reeve's house; it has been the premises of Outram's the saddlers for 150 years.

Blighs Hotel in the High Street has had an interesting history. Prior to 1828, this timber framed 16th century building was an asylum for the insane rented by the Bethlehem (Bedlam) Hospital in London. Later it became a farmhouse and was known as Bethlehem Farm, a real working farm until the early years of this century. It was purchased in 1852 by a Mr Bligh, who ran the Holmesdale Brewery. He began to let rooms in the northern part of the farmhouse, a venture that developed into the present hotel.

Included among these pictures are two early photographs of the Constitutional Club on the Vine. This building of 1889-90, which still stands, had smoking and committee rooms, a billiards room and refreshment bar. Its original use was for social and political meetings, but recently it has been used as offices. The foundation stone had been laid by Lord Cranbourne in April 1889, not in its present position on the east side of the building, but at the front where a door has subsequently been inserted.

HIGH STREET
1900 44904

An evocative traffic-free view of the fountain and the junction of High
Street and London Road. The building at the junction, the Sevenoaks
Coffee Tavern, later became the West End Dairy, before being replaced
by the present Midland Bank. The tile hung building on the left, the
former Archbishop's Reeve's house, still stands and for the past century
and a half has been the premises of Outram's the saddlers.

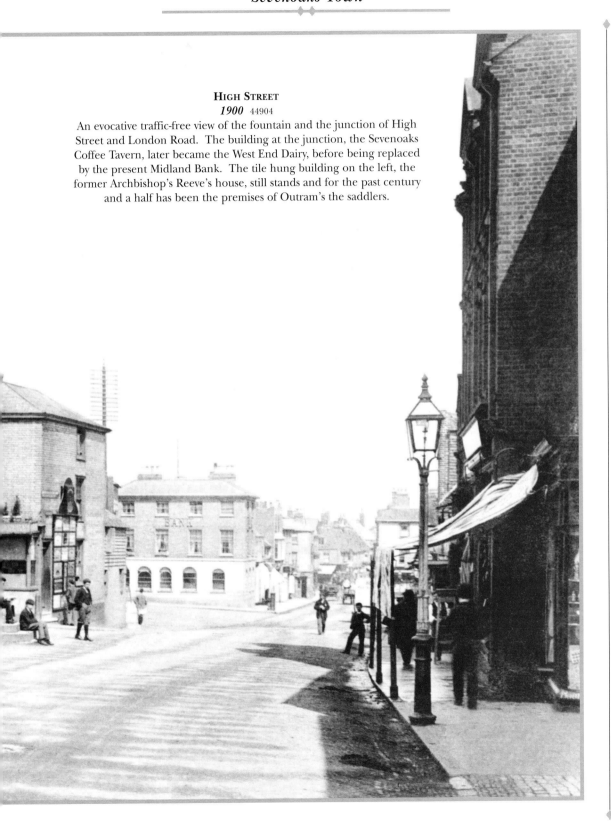

HIGH STREET c1965 S98116

The same scene some sixty years later. Outram's facade is visible on the far left, but the central building has been replaced by the Midland bank of 1922-23. The fountain, its single gas lamp replaced by more ornate electric lights, is also adorned with traffic signs.

TOWN CENTRE c1965 S98081

Looking down the High Street from the fountain. This spot has been an important focal point in the town from earliest times. During the First World War buglers of units stationed in Sevenoaks would sound Reveille and the Last Post here.

HIGH STREET C1965 S98095
A fine view of the Midland bank building at the junction of London Road and the High Street. The Sevenoaks cattle market took place in the High Street weekly on a Saturday from the Middle Ages until 1925.

HIGH STREET AND CHURCH 1900 44905

Looking across the Upper High Street from Sevenoaks School towards the tower of St Nicholas' church. This is a typically Kentish scene, with the church tower rising above attractive tile-hung cottages. The building in the centre is The Chantry, an attractive red brick house of late-17th century date.

HIGH STREET c1955 S98008

An evocative view of the small Saturday market in the High Street which continues a tradition going back some 700 years. Note the parked cars.

HIGH STREET c1960 S98065
An almost deserted High Street. It is a real period piece: note Timothy White's on the right and Freeman Hardy Willis on the left, to say nothing of the Watney's 'red barrel' above the inn sign.

UPPER HIGH STREET c1955 S98059
Rayley's Corner on Upper High Street on a quiet summer's afternoon. Six Bells Lane descends steeply on the right past the baker's shop, originally the Six Bells Alehouse.

UPPER HIGH STREET
c1955 S98057
Looking north at Rayley's Corner with the former Six Bells alehouse on the left. This is a timber framed building dating from the 16th century; the dormer windows were added in Victorian times.

UPPER HIGH STREET c1960 S98067
Another view looking north in Upper High Street with the Midland Bank building visible in the centre of the picture. On the right is the mock-Tudor Bricklayers Arms - now a private house - which was once the headquarters of the Sevenoaks Rifle Volunteers.

THE VINE 1900

A deserted Dartford Road on the west of the Vine, pictured in Spring sunlight a century ago. The Vine, the triangular shaped piece of land between the Dartford Road and Seal Hollow Road, is named after the Archbishop's vineyard which used to stand here.

THE VINE c1960

The same view as in the previous picture, but some sixty years later. At first glance little seems to have changed, save the traffic and the street lighting. Close inspection shows that the magnificent trees on the right have been severely lopped, one of the houses on the left has been extended and, most significantly, the War memorial of 1920 is visible to the right of the centre of the picture.

THE VINE 1900   44908

THE VINE c1960   S98061

CRICKET ON THE GREEN
c1960 S98042
Cricket has been played on the Vine since the mid-18th century, and in 1734 the Vine was the site of the first cricket match to be reported in the national newspapers. The elegant red brick house in the centre is Vine House. It was built in the late 18th century.

THE VINE GREEN c1965 S98133

Another view of cricket on the Vine, this time showing on the right the bandstand and the weatherboarded cricket pavilion, which dates from the early 19th century.

SEAL HOLLOW 1900 44910

This narrow curving road, which runs downhill north eastwards from the Vine, follows the line of an early trackway along a dry valley. It was much used in coaching days and was formerly known as Locks Bottom Road. The early-19th century wall to Knole Park was built by Welsh stonemasons without mortar.

SIX BELLS LANE C1955 S98007
A picturesque corner of old Sevenoaks: looking down Six Bells Lane - also known as Parsonage Lane. This narrow alleyway, lined by 18th and 19th century cottages, descends steeply from the Upper High Street. Prior to the 1860s when piped water reached Sevenoaks there was a pump at the bottom of the lane. This survives in the courtyard of the old bakery.

THE RECREATION GROUND
1895 36407
The Vine Recreation Ground at the southern end of the Vine:
Victorian children are playing games on the bandstand presented
a year earlier by Henry Swaffield JP, one of Sevenoaks' greatest
benefactors. In the background on the left is the Baptist
church of 1886.

THE RUSTIC BRIDGE AND BANDSTAND c1955 S98046
The bandstand features again in this picture taken some sixty years later; it shows Vine Gardens, with the rustic bridge over the pond built on the site of the former Club Hall - a feature of Sevenoaks social life - which was destroyed by enemy action during the Second World War.

VINE GARDENS c1965 S98109
Another view of the rustic bridge in Vine Gardens taken some ten years after the previous photograph.

PARK GRANGE C1965 S98085

At the southern end of the Upper High Street this lodge to Park Grange blocks the original line of the old Tonbridge Road. The road was diverted to the east in the 17th century so that it did not pass the front of the big house - at that time known as Park Place. The present Park Grange, now part of Sevenoaks School, was built in the 19th century. Actually, this sharp bend in the road adds much charm to the Upper High Street.

THE CONSTITUTIONAL CLUB 1895 36399

Little changed today, save that it is now offices, the club at the southern end of the Vine is pictured five years after its opening in 1890. On the right is the adjoining Club Hall, much used for dances until its destruction by a bomb in 1940.

HIGH STREET AND THE CONSTITUTIONAL CLUB
1900 44906

Another view of the Constitutional Club, this time including the drinking trough and gas lamp standard. The building on the right is the old police station. It opened in 1864 and was decommissioned in 1972. It is currently being converted into apartments.

ST NICHOLAS' CHURCH c1960 S98063

The Upper High Street entrance to the parish church of Sevenoaks with its battlemented aisles and tall west tower. It was originally built in the 13th century and extensively rebuilt in the 15th century. It has been restored on several occasions, notably in 1812, when the cost was the for those days astronomical sum of about £10,000, and again in 1878.

THE PARISH CHURCH, INTERIOR 1895 36402

An evocative century-old view of the nave of the church showing the 13th century arcades and the plaster ceiling of the 1812 restoration, which was replaced in the 1950s.

PARISH CHURCH OF ST NICHOLAS c1965 S98112
A good view of the tower of St Nicholas' church, which rises in three stages to its battlemented top and north east turret. Between 1616 and 1631 the poet John Donne was Rector here. As was frequently the case in those days he was an absentee rector and the vicar, William Turner, performed all the parochial duties.

THE BAPTIST CHAPEL 1895 36406

THE BAPTIST CHAPEL 1895
A Victorian picture of the Baptist church on the northern side of the Vine. It was built in 1886 on the site of the cottage that had been Emily Jackson's first hospital.

◆

THE COTTAGE HOSPITAL 1895
This shows the Sevenoaks and Holmesdale Cottage Hospital as it was originally built in 1873, when it had eight beds and one nurse and was funded by voluntary contributions. The hospital was enlarged in 1904 and completely rebuilt in 1921/22. A children's ward was added in 1935.

THE COTTAGE HOSPITAL 1895 36408

THE SCHOOL C1965 S98086
The Upper High Street facade of Sevenoaks School, with the figure of William Sevenoke gazing benevolently from his niche. It is interesting that Sevenoke's will, under which the school was endowed, stipulated that the school-master should not be a priest.

THE SCHOOL c1965 S98093

Another view of the High Street facade of Sevenoaks School, with an interesting array of 1960s vehicles parked in the forecourt. Sevenoaks was one of the earliest grammar schools in England.

THE GRAMMAR SCHOOL 1895 36403

The 18th-century buildings of Sevenoaks School pictured a century ago. These classic buildings, which replaced the original fabric, are thought to have been designed by Lord Burlington. The school was founded in 1432 by William Sevenoke, reputedly a foundling of the town, who prospered and became Mayor of London in 1419.

Around Sevenoaks

SEVENOAKS is a hilltop town and north and south are excellent views across the beautiful countryside of the 'Garden of England', that fitting title by which fruitful Kent has for long been known. To the north, the view expands across the sinuous Vale of Holmesdale, today tracked by the thunderous M26, to the wooded chalk escarpment of the North Downs. To the south, across the modern by-pass, lies the clay Weald rising in the blue distance to the sandstone heights of Ashdown Forest. The pictures here give a retrospective taste of this corner of Kent in the days before the big roads. They also give us glimpses of former open views within Sevenoaks itself, such as looking towards the town from Kippington Park and towards the church from Oakhill Road. Here also is a famous picture of the seven mighty oaks which once stood on the south of the town near the White Hart.

Kippington House, once the home of the scholar Thomas Farnaby who sailed with Drake on his last voyage, was rebuilt in 1780. It was at one time in the hands of the Austen family - relatives of Jane - and was turned into flats in the 1980s. Here are photographs from the Victorian era, showing its park and Kippington church taken when the church was not yet twenty years old.

Within the built-up area of Sevenoaks are some interesting 1960s pictures of St John's Hill, on the north of the town, with its row of small shops and its big Congregational Church.

Knole, the great house in its enormous deer park on the eastern side of Sevenoaks, stands aloof and independent of the town. Indeed, Knole has itself been described as 'a town rather than a house'. Its original medieval buildings were sold in 1456 to the then Archbishop of Canterbury who built the present splendid palace in their place. This eventually passed to Thomas Sackville, earl of Dorset, who embellished it in a fine display of Jacobean grandeur. Given to the National Trust in 1946, it is still the home of the Sackvilles.

Possibly the most unusual photographs of the environs of Sevenoaks in this collection are those of Woodlands Holiday Camp north of Kemsing. The holiday camp shut down in the 1960s and its terraced site is now occupied by the houses of Tinkerpot Rise. It was associated with the weekend huts which in the middle years of the 20th century lay all along the adjacent Knatts Valley. These photographs were presumably taken as promotional material in the 1950s, and show the chalets and buildings of the now-vanished complex tucked into the wooded valley in the North Downs. The spot is still remote and difficult to find, which may explain the failure of attempts in the 1970s to turn it into a night-club, to say nothing of dark rumours that it was at one time a nudist camp. Woodlands is now known for its golf course, which has developed substantially in the 1990s.

VIEW OF THE WEALD C1965 S98105

An evocative view looking southwards towards the High Weald and Ashdown Forest, with the village of Sevenoaks Weald in the middle ground. Today this tranquil scene with its clumps of trees and grazing cattle is cut by Sevenoaks by-pass.

THE SEVEN OAKS 1900 44909

This magnificent row of oak trees was planted near the White Hart inn alongside the Tonbridge turnpike road in 1727, the first row of seven oaks deliberately planted at Sevenoaks. They were felled in 1955; it was mistakenly thought that they were diseased.

VIEW FROM KIPPINGTON PARK 1895
Unrecognisable today, this view looking eastwards to Sevenoaks has been completely built over.

◆

KNOLE c1955
The greatest of Sevenoaks' great houses, magnificent Knole is set in 1,000 acres of parkland. It has been said that the house possesses 'a courtyard for every day of the week, a staircase for every week of the year and a room for every day of the year'.

VIEW FROM KIPPINGTON PARK 1895 36409

KNOLE c1955 S98002

KNOLE, THE LODGE GATES c1955 S98001
Knole is administered by the National Trust, to whom it wa
given in 1946. The park is always open to the public, an
expanse of grassland with herds of red and fallow deer and
great avenues of beech, chestnut and oak trees.

ST MARY'S, KIPPINGTON 1895 36411
Dating from 1878-80, this big towered church was built on land belonging to W J Thompson, owner of the Kippington estate, who had quarrelled with the Rector of St Nicholas' parish church. St Mary's cost him £12,500 to build. The font is thought to be a replica of one in Florence cathedral.

VIEW FROM OAK HILL 1895 36410
An intriguing view looking towards the tower of St Nicholas' church, and probably taken from Oakhill Road. The intervening land has since been built over.

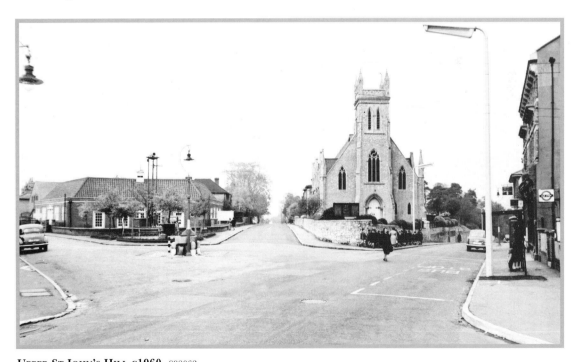

UPPER ST JOHN'S HILL c1960 S98062
An increase of traffic is the most notable change in this view today. St John's Hill Congregational Church of 1858-9 originally possessed an ungainly spire, which was removed in 1880 because it destabilised the church fabric.

St John's c1965 S98056
Goods for sale crowd onto the pavement and shoppers browse in the
sun in this 1950s picture of St John's. The only vehicles in sight are
two parked cars.

WOODLANDS C1955 S98019
A pastoral scene showing this small community tucked in a hollow of the North Downs, with the church and gabled vicarage of 1852 on the right and the older manor house hidden behind the trees. Today this view is dominated by the golf course, which covers much of the land on the left of the picture.

WOODLANDS HOLIDAY CAMP c1955 S98031
The simple delights of generations of 'hoppers' lived on at Woodlands Holiday Camp, built on its terraced site above the little church. The camp closed in the 1960s and was for a time a night club. The site has since been developed.

WOODLANDS HOLIDAY CAMP, THE RECREATION ROOM c1955 S98038
The club's recreation room, deserted save for the summer sunlight streaming in through the skylights. The furnishings are probably best described as minimalist. The room itself speaks of a now vanished era.

WOODLANDS HOLIDAY CAMP, THE CHALETS c1955 S98016
Campers pictured in the summer sun outside the 'basic' chalets - just a single cubicle of a room - which were ranged along the woodland terraces.

WOODLANDS HOLIDAY CAMP, THE SWIMMING POOL c1955 S98011
The steep terraced site looking across the swimming pool, with onlookers watching the bathers.

WOODLANDS HOLIDAY CAMP, THE SWIMMING POOL c1955 S98014

A closer look at the swimming pool and swimmers at the poolside. Is this possibly a swimming lesson? The spectators on the bench to the left certainly seem to be encouraging the small person in the life belt.

WOODLANDS HOLIDAY CAMP, THE SWIMMING POOL c1955 S98009

In the earlier days of the camp the swimming pool was open to the elements, as shown here on a warm summer's day, but it was covered in during the 1960s. In this view plenty of campers are just enjoying the sun from the comfort of a deckchair by the pool.

Tonbridge High Street

IN PHOTOGRAPHING Tonbridge High Street Frith's photographers ranged both north and south of the River Medway, including the historic part of the road and the more recent developments. The busy High Street, which follows the line of the London-Rye road, is relatively modern south of the Great Bridge, but is an interesting mixture of medieval and Tudor half-timber, Georgian and Victorian brickwork and 20th-century concrete to the north.

One of the most famous buildings in Tonbridge High Street is the old Chequers Inn, which stands close to the castle on the north side of the river. This half-timbered building dates from the 15th century and several pictures of it are included here. In 1907 it was described as 'strikingly picturesque from the street', as indeed it is still. The two gables both have cusped bargeboards. The inn is well known for its 'gallows' sign, projecting over the street, and said to have been erected originally during the reign of Elizabeth I. Tradition claims that the inn was founded in the 1520s after the suppression of the priory that had formerly offered hospitality to travellers in the town. Next door to the Chequers is another 15th century half-timbered house with magnificent curved corner braces. It has for long been in use as a shop. This area outside the Chequers, just up the hill from the Big Bridge (which itself was paid for by Henry VIII), was the original market place. Here cattle were sold in a weekly mar-

ket. It was also the site of the stocks and whipping post. The photographs included here show the Chequers' virtually unchanging facade as a backdrop to nearly a century of change: change in fashions, change in transport, change in the whole fabric of day to day life itself.

Other notable buildings which appear in these photographs include the old Public Hall, in the northern part of the High Street. This Victorian pile was built in 1874 and until recently remained a High Street landmark. It burned down in the late 1990s and is now derelict and awaiting its fate. It has served as a venue for public meetings and later as a cinema, a bingo hall and a furniture store.

South of the River Medway and close to the railway bridge stood the Angel Hotel. This handsome Georgian building occupied the corner of High Street and Vale Road and was originally a coaching inn. It was demolished in the early 1970s to make way for a roundabout and the Angel Leisure Centre. Tonbridge's architecture is the poorer for its loss, for it was both imposing and elegant, as these photographs show. Opposite the site of the Angel is the library, built in 1900 as a 'free Public Library and Technical Institute'.

The High Street is a busy shopping centre, and has been so for a century and more, as shown by these pictures. It remains the lively thoroughfare that Frith's photographers found when the Victorian era had still over a decade to run.

HIGH STREET 1890 T1015001

Looking up the High Street on a warm sunny day over a century ago. There is hardly any wheeled traffic and the crowds of shoppers themselves are a well dressed bunch - note the lady with a parasol on the left. The atmosphere of this warm day is conveyed by the open first and second floor windows and the big awnings keeping the sun from the shopfronts.

HIGH STREET 1890 T1015004

A wonderfully busy view of the High Street looking towards the Big Bridge outside the famous Chequers, with wagon and jolly wagoner, assorted carts and shouting boys. The cattle drinking trough on the extreme right is shown in its original position. It now stands south of the Chequers. Gunner's the drapers continued to trade until recently.

HIGH STREET
1890 T1015007
Another view in the pre-internal combustion engine days, looking south along the High Street with the Public Hall of 1874 on the right, before its roofline was changed. The hall burned down in the 1990s and is now derelict. Note how very muddy the street itself appears, with the dry 'paved sidewalks' to keep pedestrians dryshod.

THE CHEQUERS 1948 T101007
The famous 15th-century half-timbered Chequers Hotel and adjoining 15th-century building. The National Westminster bank stands partly on the site of the old town hall, demolished in 1901 when the road was widened. Tonbridge's old market place was in the High Street in front of the Chequers.

YE OLD CHEQUERS INN C1950 T101037

This evocative view of the Chequers was taken shortly after the Second World War. The inn is renowned for its big 'gallows' sign, which in this picture advertises only the brewer. The cars and the bicycle propped up on the kerb tell of less traffic-hassled days.

HIGH STREET 1948 T101021

Looking up a blissfully traffic-free High Street a few years after the close of the Second World War. The old Public Hall stands on the left, in those days serving as a cinema. The antiques shop opposite was established on the site in 1735 and still exists.

HIGH STREET
1948 T101004
The types of cars and motorbike with helmet-less rider show this
picture of the High Street to be over fifty years old, though apart from
a few minor details the High Street itself has changed little
in that time.

HIGH STREET 1948 T101020
Here we are looking up the High Street past the now-derelict Public Hall, with a few people waiting on its steps.
The Ivy House inn at the junction with Bordyke is visible just to the right of the bus.

HIGH STREET 1948 T101003
Burton's has gone, but its Ionic pilastered building remains, as do so many of the buildings in Tonbridge High Street, photographed here thronged with shoppers on a summer's day fifty years ago.

LONDON ROAD c1950 T101033

LONDON ROAD c1950

Looking north at the junction of London Road and Shipbourne Road opposite Tonbridge School. The picture looks across the line of the proposed relief road. The public house has gone, as have some of the buildings on the right.

HIGH STREET c1950

Looking up the High Street from the entrance to the Chequers, a scene little changed today save for the increase in traffic and the shortened gallows sign outside the hotel, which now gives only the hostelry's name.

HIGH STREET c1950 T101038

HIGH STREET 1951 T101061

Jostling crowds on the pavement half a century ago, a few parked cars, a bus and a lady on a bicycle: and yet very recognisably Tonbridge High Street, though the clock on the left has now gone.

HIGH STREET c1960 T101065

The gracious old Angel Hotel and the High Street photographed from the railway bridge. The Angel was demolished in the 1970s to make way for the Angel Centre, a shopping and leisure complex.

HIGH STREET
c1950 T101014
Looking straight up the busy High Street from the railway bridge
with the Angel Hotel on the right and the public library on the
left. To the left of the Angel is the old congregational church
which, like the Angel, was demolished in the 1970s.
The modern Christ Church now occupies the site.

HIGH STREET c1960 T101100
Another view of the High Street, this time taken about forty years ago. Since this picture was taken very little has changed; the most noticeable differences are today's endless stream of traffic and the loss of the clock on the left.

Around Tonbridge

TONBRIDGE stands on the River Medway about 120 feet above sea level. It lies in the heart of the 'Garden of England', an affectionate nickname for Kent which supplied perishables, in particular fruit, to the London market. During the 19th and early 20th centuries it was a great centre for hop production, with the tall trailing plants grown up frameworks of poles in numerous 'hop gardens'. The bines - trailing stems - have to be cut down so that the 'hops' can be picked off. Today this work is done by machinery; in earlier years it was all done by the hand labour of a vast influx of seasonal workers, particularly from London's East End, who took a working holiday 'hopping' in September. The picture of hop washing in a 'garden' near Tonbridge sets the scene to perfection.

Tonbridge has sprawled outwards since the Victorian era, and the charming photograph of Barden Park, now entirely built over, shows the cultivated rurality to be found close to the town centre in those days.

Within the town itself, standing back from the High Street, is Tonbridge Castle, a big fort that was founded soon after the Norman Conquest. Its overlord was the Archbishop of Canterbury, under whom it was held originally by the de Clare family, the last of whom, Gilbert, was killed at the Battle of Bannockburn in 1314. A later lord of the castle was the Duke of Buckingham, who was executed for high treason in 1520. The mighty Norman keep was destroyed after the Civil War. The castle's solid 13th century gate-house is pictured here in the middle years of the 20th century, set within its leafy municipal gardens. The castle was built in a fine strategic position to guard the point where the road from London, which was beginning to supplant Winchester in importance, crossed the Medway on its way to the Channel ports of Rye and Winchelsea. In early days travellers would have forded the river but later, probably by the early 14th century, a bridge was built on the site of the present Big Bridge. At that time the bridge was known as the Town Bridge; it has also been called Great Bridge and Principal Bridge. This medieval bridge fell into disrepair and was replaced in 1526 by a new stone bridge financed by Henry VIII. This too fell into disrepair, and was replaced in 1775 by a rather elegant structure that was carried away by floods in 1814. The brick bridge that replaced the 1775 one was strengthened in the 1880s by the replacement of the picturesque brick arches with cast iron beams. These in turn have been replaced by steel ones.

The old parish church of St Peter and St Paul stands back from the High Street. It is a large building of local sandstone dating originally from Norman times. Strangely, there are no memorials to the de Clare family, the builders of the castle, or its subsequent inhabitants. This is probably because when the church was extensively restored and rebuilt, in particular in the 1870s, any monuments to them were removed.

THE PARISH CHURCH OF ST PETER AND ST PAUL 1948 T101013
A wedding car stands outside the parish church of St Peter and St Paul on this sunny afternoon over half a century ago. The picture was taken looking along Church Lane, one of the ancient streets of Tonbridge, towards the medieval parish church.

THE PLAYING FIELDS c1950 T101034

Tonbridge School is well known for its cricketing tradition. Here the wide expanse of the school's playing fields is shown against a backdrop of the school's main 19th-century buildings. To the left of the tree is the chapel of 1902 which burnt down in 1989 and has since been rebuilt.

TONBRIDGE SCHOOL c1955 T101062

The main buildings of Tonbridge School, set back from the High Street, form an E-shaped block in local sandstone. The school, founded under a charter of 1553, remained a local grammar school until its rapid development in the 19th century.

THE CASTLE 1948 T101011

The outer side of the great 13th-century gatehouse, the best surviving part of Tonbridge Castle. This massive building of yellow sandstone is pictured in summer sunlight over fifty years ago. The Norman keep which crowned the nearby earthen motte, and was besieged by William II in 1088, was destroyed by Parliamentary forces during the Civil War.

THE CASTLE c1950

Another mid-20th century view of the 13th century gatehouse, this time looking north. The adjoining building on the right, now municipal offices, was built in 1793. Part of the remaining curtain wall can be seen on the left.

◆

THE CASTLE 1951

A further view of the southern, internal, side of the gatehouse, with the lawn enclosed within the original castle precincts. This photograph exudes a sense of peace and well-being, as spectators turn to watch the small child, just right of centre, and the dog playing on the lawn.

THE CASTLE c1950 T101078

THE CASTLE 1951 T101044

THE CASTLE GARDENS 1951 T101047
The present castle gardens were at one time 'Mr Hooker's vinery', Thomas Hooker being an 18th-century owner of the site. In 1897-98 the local authority purchased the estate, and took full possession in 1900.

THE WATER GATES 1890 T1015002

The Medway was a recreational river by late Victorian times; here, rowing skiffs are shown for hire just up river from the Big Bridge, from which this picture was taken. This is the most recent bridge to be built at this spot, which is close to the original ford that the castle was built to guard.

THE RIVER MEDWAY 1890 T1015008

A tranquil River Medway. Until the coming of the turnpike roads and, later, the railways, the Medway was Kent's great highway, with locks constructed from Maidstone to Tonbridge by 1739.

THE BRIDGE
1890 T1015005
The Big Bridge and the River Medway over a hundred years ago, with rowing skiffs on the left of the picture. The bridge was widened in 1887-88 and again in 1925-27. The building on the right with its quirky little turret was originally a bank but is now a pizzeria.

RIVERSIDE GARDENS 1948 T101008
Looking downriver from the gardens beside the castle on a summer's day shortly after the Second World War. This pleasant place to stroll has changed little in fifty years.

THE RIVER AND THE BRIDGE 1951 T101042
Looking across the River Medway and the Big Bridge to the boat hire point at the water gates. The original stone bridge on this site was built in 1526; it was replaced in 1775 by a bridge that was destroyed by flooding in 1814. A new brick bridge was built, but in the 1880s the arches were replaced by cast iron beams, which have now been replaced by steel girders.

THE BRIDGE
1951 T101074
The Big Bridge and a tranquil Medway. Today the bridge is usually known as the Big Bridge, but it has been called by various names, including Town Bridge, Great Bridge and Principal Bridge.

THE RIVER MEDWAY c1950 T101031
A couple take their leisure in an old fashioned rowing skiff on the River Medway. The river has a long history of human use and was known as the Fluminus Meduwaeias to the Romans and as the Medwaeg, the 'sweet river', to the Saxons.

THE RIVER MEDWAY c1950 T101030
Another tranquil river scene. Looking at this, it is hard to believe that the Medway at Tonbridge has been notorious for flooding with disastrous results, as recently as 1968. The new flood defence scheme with its barrier and designated flood storage area should preserve central Tonbridge from flooding in the future.

BARDEN PARK, THE AVENUE 1890 T1015003

A charming picture of a vanished scene, for Barden Park is no more, built over in the early and middle years of the 20th century. Here, amid the trees two little girls await a horse and trap driven by some ladies.

QUARRY HILL 1890 T1015006

Another lost sight, since Quarry Hill is now on the edge of the Tonbridge by-pass to the south of the town. Here two Victorian men push their bicycles uphill, followed by a small boy in strange headgear. On the right is a parked bicycle and a seated cyclist.

HOP WASHING
1890 T1015009
Tonbridge was in the centre of the hop garden area of Kent;
this picture illustrates the hard manual labour required in
the production of hops.

Index

Frith Book Co Titles

www.francisfrith.co.uk

The Frith Book Company publishes over 100 new titles each year. A selection of those currently available are listed below. For latest catalogue please contact Frith Book Co.

Town Books 96 pages, approx 100 photos. County and Themed Books 128 pages, approx 150 photos (unless specified). All titles hardback laminated case and jacket except those indicated pb (paperback)

Amersham, Chesham & Rickmansworth (pb)			Derby (pb)	1-85937-367-4	£9.99
	1-85937-340-2	£9.99	Derbyshire (pb)	1-85937-196-5	£9.99
Ancient Monuments & Stone Circles	1-85937-143-4	£17.99	Devon (pb)	1-85937-297-x	£9.99
Aylesbury (pb)	1-85937-227-9	£9.99	Dorset (pb)	1-85937-269-4	£9.99
Bakewell	1-85937-113-2	£12.99	Dorset Churches	1-85937-172-8	£17.99
Barnstaple (pb)	1-85937-300-3	£9.99	Dorset Coast (pb)	1-85937-299-6	£9.99
Bath (pb)	1-85937-419-0	£9.99	Dorset Living Memories	1-85937-210-4	£14.99
Bedford (pb)	1-85937-205-8	£9.99	Down the Severn	1-85937-118-3	£14.99
Berkshire (pb)	1-85937-191-4	£9.99	Down the Thames (pb)	1-85937-278-3	£9.99
Berkshire Churches	1-85937-170-1	£17.99	Down the Trent	1-85937-311-9	£14.99
Blackpool (pb)	1-85937-382-8	£9.99	Dublin (pb)	1-85937-231-7	£9.99
Bognor Regis (pb)	1-85937-431-x	£9.99	East Anglia (pb)	1-85937-265-1	£9.99
Bournemouth	1-85937-067-5	£12.99	East London	1-85937-080-2	£14.99
Bradford (pb)	1-85937-204-x	£9.99	East Sussex	1-85937-130-2	£14.99
Brighton & Hove(pb)	1-85937-192-2	£8.99	Eastbourne	1-85937-061-6	£12.99
Bristol (pb)	1-85937-264-3	£9.99	Edinburgh (pb)	1-85937-193-0	£8.99
British Life A Century Ago (pb)	1-85937-213-9	£9.99	England in the 1880s	1-85937-331-3	£17.99
Buckinghamshire (pb)	1-85937-200-7	£9.99	English Castles (pb)	1-85937-434-4	£9.99
Camberley (pb)	1-85937-222-8	£9.99	English Country Houses	1-85937-161-2	£17.99
Cambridge (pb)	1-85937-422-0	£9.99	Essex (pb)	1-85937-270-8	£9.99
Cambridgeshire (pb)	1-85937-420-4	£9.99	Exeter	1-85937-126-4	£12.99
Canals & Waterways (pb)	1-85937-291-0	£9.99	Exmoor	1-85937-132-9	£14.99
Canterbury Cathedral (pb)	1-85937-179-5	£9.99	Falmouth	1-85937-066-7	£12.99
Cardiff (pb)	1-85937-093-4	£9.99	Folkestone (pb)	1-85937-124-8	£9.99
Carmarthenshire	1-85937-216-3	£14.99	Glasgow (pb)	1-85937-190-6	£9.99
Chelmsford (pb)	1-85937-310-0	£9.99	Gloucestershire	1-85937-102-7	£14.99
Cheltenham (pb)	1-85937-095-0	£9.99	Great Yarmouth (pb)	1-85937-426-3	£9.99
Cheshire (pb)	1-85937-271-6	£9.99	Greater Manchester (pb)	1-85937-266-x	£9.99
Chester	1-85937-090-x	£12.99	Guildford (pb)	1-85937-410-7	£9.99
Chesterfield	1-85937-378-x	£9.99	Hampshire (pb)	1-85937-279-1	£9.99
Chichester (pb)	1-85937-228-7	£9.99	Hampshire Churches (pb)	1-85937-207-4	£9.99
Colchester (pb)	1-85937-188-4	£8.99	Harrogate	1-85937-423-9	£9.99
Cornish Coast	1-85937-163-9	£14.99	Hastings & Bexhill (pb)	1-85937-131-0	£9.99
Cornwall (pb)	1-85937-229-5	£9.99	Heart of Lancashire (pb)	1-85937-197-3	£9.99
Cornwall Living Memories	1-85937-248-1	£14.99	Helston (pb)	1-85937-214-7	£9.99
Cotswolds (pb)	1-85937-230-9	£9.99	Hereford (pb)	1-85937-175-2	£9.99
Cotswolds Living Memories	1-85937-255-4	£14.99	Herefordshire	1-85937-174-4	£14.99
County Durham	1-85937-123-x	£14.99	Hertfordshire (pb)	1-85937-247-3	£9.99
Croydon Living Memories	1-85937-162-0	£9.99	Horsham (pb)	1-85937-432-8	£9.99
Cumbria	1-85937-101-9	£14.99	Humberside	1-85937-215-5	£14.99
Dartmoor	1-85937-145-0	£14.99	Hythe, Romney Marsh & Ashford	1-85937-256-2	£9.99

Available from your local bookshop or from the publisher

Frith Book Co Titles (continued)

Ipswich (pb)	1-85937-424-7	£9.99	St Ives (pb)	1-85937415-8	£9.99
Ireland (pb)	1-85937-181-7	£9.99	Scotland (pb)	1-85937-182-5	£9.99
Isle of Man (pb)	1-85937-268-6	£9.99	Scottish Castles (pb)	1-85937-323-2	£9.99
Isles of Scilly	1-85937-136-1	£14.99	Sevenoaks & Tunbridge	1-85937-057-8	£12.99
Isle of Wight (pb)	1-85937-429-8	£9.99	Sheffield, South Yorks (pb)	1-85937-267-8	£9.99
Isle of Wight Living Memories	1-85937-304-6	£14.99	Shrewsbury (pb)	1-85937-325-9	£9.99
Kent (pb)	1-85937-189-2	£9.99	Shropshire (pb)	1-85937-326-7	£9.99
Kent Living Memories	1-85937-125-6	£14.99	Somerset	1-85937-153-1	£14.99
Lake District (pb)	1-85937-275-9	£9.99	South Devon Coast	1-85937-107-8	£14.99
Lancaster, Morecambe & Heysham (pb)	1-85937-233-3	£9.99	South Devon Living Memories	1-85937-168-x	£14.99
Leeds (pb)	1-85937-202-3	£9.99	South Hams	1-85937-220-1	£14.99
Leicester	1-85937-073-x	£12.99	Southampton (pb)	1-85937-427-1	£9.99
Leicestershire (pb)	1-85937-185-x	£9.99	Southport (pb)	1-85937-425-5	£9.99
Lincolnshire (pb)	1-85937-433-6	£9.99	Staffordshire	1-85937-047-0	£12.99
Liverpool & Merseyside (pb)	1-85937-234-1	£9.99	Stratford upon Avon	1-85937-098-5	£12.99
London (pb)	1-85937-183-3	£9.99	Suffolk (pb)	1-85937-221-x	£9.99
Ludlow (pb)	1-85937-176-0	£9.99	Suffolk Coast	1-85937-259-7	£14.99
Luton (pb)	1-85937-235-x	£9.99	Surrey (pb)	1-85937-240-6	£9.99
Maidstone	1-85937-056-x	£14.99	Sussex (pb)	1-85937-184-1	£9.99
Manchester (pb)	1-85937-198-1	£9.99	Swansea (pb)	1-85937-167-1	£9.99
Middlesex	1-85937-158-2	£14.99	Tees Valley & Cleveland	1-85937-211-2	£14.99
New Forest	1-85937-128-0	£14.99	Thanet (pb)	1-85937-116-7	£9.99
Newark (pb)	1-85937-366-6	£9.99	Tiverton (pb)	1-85937-178-7	£9.99
Newport, Wales (pb)	1-85937-258-9	£9.99	Torbay	1-85937-063-2	£12.99
Newquay (pb)	1-85937-421-2	£9.99	Truro	1-85937-147-7	£12.99
Norfolk (pb)	1-85937-195-7	£9.99	Victorian and Edwardian Cornwall	1-85937-252-x	£14.99
Norfolk Living Memories	1-85937-217-1	£14.99	Victorian & Edwardian Devon	1-85937-253-8	£14.99
Northamptonshire	1-85937-150-7	£14.99	Victorian & Edwardian Kent	1-85937-149-3	£14.99
Northumberland Tyne & Wear (pb)	1-85937-281-3	£9.99	Vic & Ed Maritime Album	1-85937-144-2	£17.99
North Devon Coast	1-85937-146-9	£14.99	Victorian and Edwardian Sussex	1-85937-157-4	£14.99
North Devon Living Memories	1-85937-261-9	£14.99	Victorian & Edwardian Yorkshire	1-85937-154-x	£14.99
North London	1-85937-206-6	£14.99	Victorian Seaside	1-85937-159-0	£17.99
North Wales (pb)	1-85937-298-8	£9.99	Villages of Devon (pb)	1-85937-293-7	£9.99
North Yorkshire (pb)	1-85937-236-8	£9.99	Villages of Kent (pb)	1-85937-294-5	£9.99
Norwich (pb)	1-85937-194-9	£8.99	Villages of Sussex (pb)	1-85937-295-3	£9.99
Nottingham (pb)	1-85937-324-0	£9.99	Warwickshire (pb)	1-85937-203-1	£9.99
Nottinghamshire (pb)	1-85937-187-6	£9.99	Welsh Castles (pb)	1-85937-322-4	£9.99
Oxford (pb)	1-85937-411-5	£9.99	West Midlands (pb)	1-85937-289-9	£9.99
Oxfordshire (pb)	1-85937-430-1	£9.99	West Sussex	1-85937-148-5	£14.99
Peak District (pb)	1-85937-280-5	£9.99	West Yorkshire (pb)	1-85937-201-5	£9.99
Penzance	1-85937-069-1	£12.99	Weymouth (pb)	1-85937-209-0	£9.99
Peterborough (pb)	1-85937-219-8	£9.99	Wiltshire (pb)	1-85937-277-5	£9.99
Piers	1-85937-237-6	£17.99	Wiltshire Churches (pb)	1-85937-171-x	£9.99
Plymouth	1-85937-119-1	£12.99	Wiltshire Living Memories	1-85937-245-7	£14.99
Poole & Sandbanks (pb)	1-85937-251-1	£9.99	Winchester (pb)	1-85937-428-x	£9.99
Preston (pb)	1-85937-212-0	£9.99	Windmills & Watermills	1-85937-242-2	£17.99
Reading (pb)	1-85937-238-4	£9.99	Worcester (pb)	1-85937-165-5	£9.99
Romford (pb)	1-85937-319-4	£9.99	Worcestershire	1-85937-152-3	£14.99
Salisbury (pb)	1-85937-239-2	£9.99	York (pb)	1-85937-199-x	£9.99
Scarborough (pb)	1-85937-379-8	£9.99	Yorkshire (pb)	1-85937-186-8	£9.99
St Albans (pb)	1-85937-341-0	£9.99	Yorkshire Living Memories	1-85937-166-3	£14.99

See Frith books on the internet www.francisfrith.co.uk

FRITH PRODUCTS & SERVICES

Francis Frith would doubtless be pleased to know that the pioneering publishing venture he started in 1860 still continues today. A hundred and forty years later, The Francis Frith Collection continues in the same innovative tradition and is now one of the foremost publishers of vintage photographs in the world. Some of the current activities include:

Interior Decoration

Today Frith's photographs can be seen framed and as giant wall murals in thousands of pubs, restaurants, hotels, banks, retail stores and other public buildings throughout the country. In every case they enhance the unique local atmosphere of the places they depict and provide reminders of gentler days in an increasingly busy and frenetic world.

Product Promotions

Frith products are used by many major companies to promote the sales of their own products or to reinforce their own history and heritage. Frith promotions have been used by Hovis bread, Courage beers, Scots Porage Oats, Colman's mustard, Cadbury's foods, Mellow Birds coffee, Dunhill pipe tobacco, Guinness, and Bulmer's Cider.

Genealogy and Family History

As the interest in family history and roots grows world-wide, more and more people are turning to Frith's photographs of Great Britain for images of the towns, villages and streets where their ancestors lived; and, of course, photographs of the churches and chapels where their ancestors were christened, married and buried are an essential part of every genealogy tree and family album.

Frith Products

All Frith photographs are available Framed or just as Mounted Prints and Posters (size 23 x 16 inches). These may be ordered from the address below. From time to time other products - Address Books, Calendars, Table Mats, etc - are available.

The Internet

Already twenty thousand Frith photographs can be viewed and purchased on the internet through the Frith websites and a myriad of partner sites.

For more detailed information on Frith companies and products, look at these sites:

www.francisfrith.co.uk
www.francisfrith.com
(for North American visitors)

See the complete list of Frith Books at:

www.francisfrith.co.uk

This web site is regularly updated with the latest list of publications from the Frith Book Company. If you wish to buy books relating to another part of the country that your local bookshop does not stock, you may purchase on-line.

For further information, trade, or author enquiries please contact us at the address below:
The Francis Frith Collection, Frith's Barn, Teffont, Salisbury, Wiltshire, England SP3 5QP.
Tel: +44 (0)1722 716 376 Fax: +44 (0)1722 716 881 Email: sales@francisfrith.co.uk

See Frith books on the internet www.francisfrith.co.uk

TO RECEIVE YOUR **FREE** MOUNTED PRINT

Mounted Print
Overall size 14 x 11 inches

Cut out this Voucher and return it with your remittance for £1.95 to cover postage and handling, to UK addresses. For overseas addresses please include £4.00 post and handling. Choose any photograph included in this book. Your SEPIA print will be A4 in size, and mounted in a cream mount with burgundy rule line, overall size 14 x 11 inches.

Order additional Mounted Prints at HALF PRICE (only £7.49 each*)

If there are further pictures you would like to order, possibly as gifts for friends and family, purchase them at half price (no additional postage and handling required).

Have your Mounted Prints framed*

For an additional £14.95 per print you can have your chosen Mounted Print framed in an elegant polished wood and gilt moulding, overall size 16 x 13 inches (no additional postage and handling required).

---

* IMPORTANT!
These special prices are only available if ordered using the original voucher on this page (no copies permitted) and at the same time as your free Mounted Print, for delivery to the same address

---

Frith Collectors' Guild

From time to time we publish a magazine of news and stories about Frith photographs and further special offers of Frith products. If you would like 12 months FREE membership, please return this form.

Send completed forms to:
The Francis Frith Collection, Frith's Barn, Teffont, Salisbury, Wiltshire SP3 5QP

Voucher for **FREE** and Reduced Price Frith Prints

Picture no.	Page number	Qty	Mounted @ £7.49	Framed + £14.95	Total Cost
		1	**Free of charge***	£	£
			£7.49	£	£
			£7.49	£	£
			£7.49	£	£
			£7.49	£	£
			£7.49	£	£

Please allow 28 days for delivery *** Post & handling**	**£1.95**
Book Title . . . . **Total Order Cost**	**£**

Please do not photocopy this voucher. Only the original is valid, so please cut it out and return it to us.

I enclose a cheque / postal order for £ . . . .
made payable to 'The Francis Frith Collection'
OR please debit my Mastercard / Visa / Switch / Amex card
(credit cards please on all overseas orders)

Number . . . .

Issue No (Switch only) . . . . .Valid from (Amex/Switch) . . . .

Expires . . . . Signature . . . .

Name Mr/Mrs/Ms . . . .

Address . . . .

. . . .

. . . . Postcode . . . .

Daytime Tel No . . . .   Valid to 31/12/02

The Francis Frith Collectors' Guild

Please enrol me as a member for 12 months free of charge.

Name Mr/Mrs/Ms . . . .

Address . . . .

. . . .

. . . . Postcode . . . .

Would you like to find out more about Francis Frith?

We have recently recruited some entertaining speakers who are happy to visit local groups, clubs and societies to give an illustrated talk documenting Frith's travels and photographs. If you are a member of such a group and are interested in hosting a presentation, we would love to hear from you.

Our speakers bring with them a small selection of our local town and county books, together with sample prints. They are happy to take orders. A small proportion of the order value is donated to the group who have hosted the presentation. The talks are therefore an excellent way of fundraising for small groups and societies.

Can you help us with information about any of the Frith photographs in this book?

We are gradually compiling an historical record for each of the photographs in the Frith archive. It is always fascinating to find out the names of the people shown in the pictures, as well as insights into the shops, buildings and other features depicted.

If you recognize anyone in the photographs in this book, or if you have information not already included in the author's caption, do let us know. We would love to hear from you, and will try to publish it in future books or articles.

Our production team

Frith books are produced by a small dedicated team at offices in the converted Grade II listed 18th-century barn at Teffont near Salisbury, illustrated above. Most have worked with the Frith Collection for many years. All have in common one quality: they have a passion for the Frith Collection. The team is constantly expanding, but currently includes:

Jason Buck, John Buck, Douglas Burns, Heather Crisp, Isobel Hall, Rob Hames, Hazel Heaton, Peter Horne, James Kinnear, Tina Leary, Hannah Marsh, Eliza Sackett, Terence Sackett, Sandra Sanger, Shelley Tolcher, Susanna Walker, Clive Wathen and Jenny Wathen.